THE DIVIDEND
MILLIONAIRE

INVESTING FOR INCOME AND
WINNING IN THE STOCK MARKET

ALEX NKENCHOR UWAJEH

Legal Disclaimers

This book is presented to you for informational purposes only and is not a substitution for any professional advice. The contents herein are based on the views and opinions of the author and all associated contributors.

While every effort has been made by the author and all associated contributors to present accurate and up to date information within this document, it is apparent technologies rapidly change. Therefore, the author and all associated contributors reserve the right to update the contents and information provided herein as these

changes progress. The author and/or all associated contributors take no responsibility for any errors or omissions if such discrepancies exist within this document.

The author and all other contributors accept no responsibility for any consequential actions taken, whether monetary, legal, or otherwise, by any and all readers of the materials provided. It is the readers sole responsibility to seek professional advice before taking any action on their part.

Readers results will vary based on their skill level and individual perception of the contents herein, and thus no guarantees, monetarily or otherwise, can be made accurately. Therefore, no guarantees are made.

Table of Contents

Discount available for bulk buying

email:sales@247broadstreet.com

Acknowledgements

This book is lovingly dedicated to my wife, Sarah Uwajeh

Our God is fearful in praises, all honour, and glory belongs to Him.

Introduction

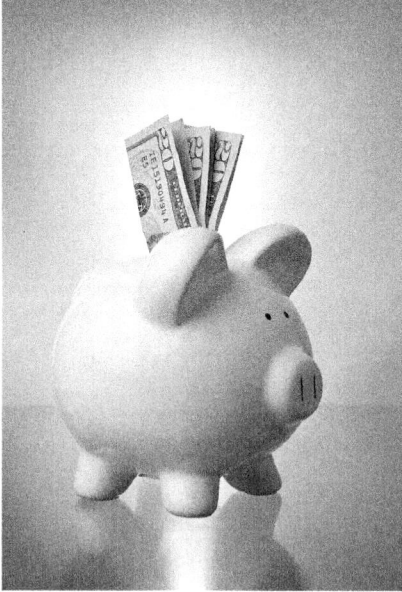

It's no secret that many people will retire without enough income to live on. Savings have dwindled to a point that simply won't sustain any type of realistic lifestyle once you stop working. If you're in this position yourself, how do you intend to pay for your expenses and lifestyle throughout your own retirement years?

More importantly, even if you're decades away from thoughts of retirement, how secure is your current income? The vast majority of people are highly dependent on the income they receive from their salary. When times are good, people don't often

think about job security. They tend to spend almost everything they earn and save very little of the money they receive.

Yet, when times aren't so good is when people tend to start thinking about ways to supplement their income or even replace it altogether. This is when thoughts of investing often spring to mind.

Investing is supposed to be all about putting aside some of your own money into an investment vehicle designed to help increase the initial amount you put into it. This is where people buy into a particular investment and hope that their initial deposit grows enough to represent a profit. This is also known as investing for capital growth.

What most people don't realize is that it's very possible to also invest to create income. When you know where you should look, it's actually easy to invest wisely in specific investment vehicles that return a steady income to you, year after year.

Imagine if you had the ability to invest in something that could bring in a regular income for you as well as grow your wealth at the same time?

That's what we'll learn in this book. You'll learn about ways to develop a strong investment portfolio that is able to grow in value automatically – if you set it up the right way. You'll also learn exactly how to turn that portfolio into an income producing investment.

Are you ready to get started? Let's get into it...

Trading or Investing?

Before you jump into the concept of investing for income, it's important to understand the vital difference between trading and investing. Think for a moment about people who buy stocks at a low price and then immediately sell when the stock price rises enough to make them a profit. This tactic is called trading. Effectively, you're putting your money into the market

and speculating that the price of the stock you bought might go up. It's a bit like gambling on the market moving in the right direction to create a profit based on your trade. The same concept is true for people who buy real estate with the plan of renovating it and then flipping it for a quick profit.

While there is nothing wrong with this form of wealth creation, it is essentially still trading.

By comparison, investing involved putting your money into a particular investment type and planning to see a solid return over the long term. This might be buying an investment property in order to benefit from the rental income you receive over the years. It might be putting money into a high-interest bearing savings account and benefiting from the interest you earn.

It may also be buying into the stock market to earn dividends on the stocks you have sitting in your portfolio over the long term.

THE DIVIDEND
MILLIONAIRE

The real key behind becoming a Dividend Millionaire is to adopt a long-term investing approach. Even if the price of your stocks increases, your goal isn't to sell them and reap the profits. Your goal is to derive income from the dividends on a healthy, growing portfolio of good quality stocks.

In order to really develop a Dividend Millionaire mindset, it's important you take a long-term view to your investing strategies and tactics.

Understanding Dividends

Dividends are payments made to shareholders of a company from the profits made and income earned by that company. When a publicly listed company earns a profit it is able to distribute some of that profit between the shareholders. Some companies may choose to retain a portion of profits to put towards future company growth.

Even if you only own one share of an enormous corporation, you stand to earn dividends from it regularly. Dividend yields are most often allocated as a fixed amount per share owned, but they aren't always necessarily paid out in cash.

Forms of Dividend Payments

Cash Dividends – A cash dividend payment is actually the most common form of payment made. This is where shareholders receive a cheque for the amount due to them. In some cases, dividends may also be

paid via electronic funds transfer directly into a bank account.

For example: if you own 100 shares and your dividend is quoted at $0.40 cents per share owned, you'll receive $40.

Scrip or Stock Dividends – Stock dividends are paid out in the form of additional stocks of that particular corporation. In most cases the stocks are issued as a proportion of any shares owned by the shareholder in that corporation.

For example: if you own 100 shares and your stock dividend is quoted at 5% reallocation, you'll receive 5 additional shares that will be added automatically to your stock portfolio.

Dividend Re-Investment – Some corporations offer a dividend re-investment option (DRIP). This is not quite the same as a Scrip or stock dividend. Instead, the issuing corporation may allow shareholders to use their dividend earnings to buy stocks to an equal value. There are also some

corporations that may offer a small discount on the stock prices for choosing this option. As stocks are added to the shareholder's portfolio automatically, there are no commissions to pay.

Property Dividends – Property dividends can be paid out by a corporation in the form of assets. This might include stocks from the corporation in which shares are owned, or even a subsidiary corporation. However, these are quite rare.

Understanding Dividend Dates

When you buy stocks, you may notice that there will be an annotation next to it in your trading account. This will be either (ex-dividend) or (cum dividend).

Depending on when you buy or sell, these annotations can have the power to affect

your trading strategy and your dividend earnings as well.

Ex-Dividend Dates

If you buy stocks that have been declared ex-dividend, they do not have the right to be paid the most recent dividend declared. However, if you sell your stocks during the ex-dividend date you still receive the most recent dividend payment due – not the new owner of those stocks.

Cum Dividend Dates

Any stock bought or sold 'cum dividend' has the right attached to it to be paid the most recently declared dividend payment.

Declaration Date

This is the date on which a corporation's Board of Directors will announce their intention to pay stockholders a dividend.

The amount of dividend paid per share is usually confirmed and a payment date is also agreed on.

Starting Small for Big Gains

The biggest reason most people never begin investing is because they believe they don't have enough money to get started. This just isn't true. It's very possible to start with very small amounts of money and you certainly can begin investing in certain stocks in order to receive a dividend yield.

You see, it is very possible buy stocks with a relatively small amount of money. The key is to know which stocks to buy that will help you increase your stock portfolio more quickly. This might be by an increase in price, or capital growth, but it may also be because of good dividend yields reinvested back into your portfolio to help you build it even faster.

The key is to get started. Period. Even if you only have $100 to invest for now, that's enough to begin. In fact, you can even find

brokerages out there that will let you start investing with just $25 per week. This doesn't sound like a lot of money, but it does have the potential to grow over time. You can always add to your stock portfolio as you start putting aside more money from your income each week to invest with.

We'll also go through some ways you can actively grow and increase your portfolio without using your own money in a later section of this book.

When most people start thinking about buying stocks on a relatively small budget, they immediately go looking for 'cheap' stocks. They seem to believe that buying 1,000 stocks at 0.10 cents per share will be better for them than buying 10 stocks at $10 per share for the same $100 investment.

Aside from this, those stocks selling at 0.10 per share might only give you a dividend yield of 2%, while the stocks selling for $10 per share might offer you a 7% dividend

yield. The key here is to consider how much you'll earn back from your initial investment, along with evaluating the issuing company for strength and stability at the same time.

Never be persuaded to buy stocks simply because they appear cheap. If you're serious about building a strong dividend income, you need to focus on quality stocks from companies that consistently perform well and show positive earnings.

Cheap vs. Discounted

Of course, there is also a big difference between 'cheap' and discounted. The stock market is notoriously volatile. Stock prices go up and down regularly. If you tend to watch market movements, you can quickly become unnerved by how frequently prices seem to change.

This is where research will pay off in the long run for you. Cheap stocks can sometimes be an indicator of a poorly performing company. By comparison,

discounted stocks may be a sign of a strong company suffering from price adjustments in a weak market.

Obviously, buying a good quality stock at a discounted price will give you far better quality stocks within your portfolio than a poor quality stock that you think seems cheap.

It's always better to look for quality stock to add to your portfolio rather than trying to shop in the bargain basement.

Cheap Stocks are Cheap for a Reason

When you see very cheap stocks selling at a few cents per share, think about how those prices may have been reached. Each individual stock is a portion of ownership of a much larger corporation. You may see extremely profitable corporations selling stocks for hundreds of dollars per share, but when you see corporations buying and

selling stocks for pennies, there's something amiss.

There's also the fact that really cheap stocks often carry much greater risks. The company itself may not be in a position to post a profit, which means you won't be earning dividends from owning those stocks. The company might be struggling with financial issues or over-burdened with debts or faltering due to poor management. Each of these things has the capacity to cause stock prices to fall dramatically, which then makes them look cheap.

Choosing the Right Stocks for Your Portfolio

The stocks you should be focused on adding to your portfolio should include good quality stocks from strong, well-performing corporations. However, those stocks should also show a decent dividend yield at the same time.

Ideally, the yield you receive should be higher than the amount you could receive from leaving your money sitting in an interest-bearing bank account. However,

always be a little wary of companies paying out extraordinarily high dividend yields.

Additionally, the price you pay for your stock should also be a consideration. Far too many investors have a belief that under-performing stocks should be a good buy opportunity. This happens when a company's share price is falling and many investors jump onto it, hoping that it may recover back up to its previous high price.

Unfortunately, there are corporations whose stock prices fall dramatically and never recover their previous high prices.

On the same note, there may also be corporations that are trading at lower-than-normal stock prices for short-term reasons. This could be an indication that the stock price may actually bounce back after that short-term under-performance.

This might seem confusing, but researching the company's trading history, profitability, debt and asset levels, and checking what previous dividend yields were like can give

you a fair indication of which stocks will be better suited to your portfolio than others.

The most important thing to look at when you're evaluating any stock is to consider the future prospects of that company. Always assess each individual stock based on the merits of the company as a whole.

You should also research the recent dividend payment history of that particular corporation. This lets you determine whether a company has demonstrated a consistency in raising the amount of dividends they pay out every year. Companies such as these are dedicated to rewarding their long-term investors, so they're not likely to decrease their dividends in future.

Remember that companies that are performing well will only boost the amounts they pay in dividends if they're performing well. If any corporation you're researching seems to have stopped raising dividends, or

actively reduced them, you should be slightly worried.

Dividend Yield Formula

Working out the dividend yield is quite easy. Take the dividend amount per share offered and divide it by the price you intend to pay.

Dividend Yield = Dividend divided by Price

As noted in the previous section, try to aim for strong, quality stocks with a good dividend yield.

Payout Ratio Formula

Another useful calculation to keep in mind is the payout ratio. The payout ratio is the amount of earnings paid out in dividends to shareholders from the issuing company. A low ratio indicates a secure dividend. This is because smaller dividends are easier for that company to pay out than larger dividend payments.

For example: if a company earns $2 per share and pays its shareholders $1 in

dividends, the ratio becomes 50%. That particular company is paying out only half its income in dividends. Yet, it's retaining the other 50% to be reinvested back into the company for future growth.

The formula for calculating a payout ratio is as follows:

Payout ratio = dividends paid out per share divided by earnings per share

So, in this example, the dividends paid out are $1 and the earnings per share are $2.

$1 divided by $2 = 0.50 or 50%

A really high payout of over 75% is cause for concern, as that company is paying out dividends to shareholders and retaining almost nothing to pay for future company growth.

Diversify Your Portfolio

When you're researching which stocks to buy, always consider a variety of sectors in which to invest. You might do all your research and learn that mining companies

or financial companies offer the best yields at reasonable prices for what you want to achieve.

But overloading your portfolio with stocks all in the same sector leaves you exposed to potential falls in your overall portfolio value if something happens to the companies within that sector.

Keep your portfolio safe by diversifying into a range of sectors. You'll find excellent companies within banking, retail, mining, IT and technology, commodities, and many others besides.

Ideally, your portfolio shouldn't contain any more than two stocks from within the same sector.

Making Money When the Market Falls

Even very strong corporations can suffer falling stock prices during market crashes. During uncertain economic times, many investors feel the need to sell off their

stocks in an effort to avoid losing money as the market falls.

Yet, smart investors understand that a strong, profitable, well-performing corporation may experience a temporary dip in prices that may well come right back once the market recovers. This is the ideal time to buy very strong stocks with decent dividend yields at a discounted price.

When you do your dividend yield calculations during these conditions, you should notice they appear a little better than normal. This is because the initial stock price is reduced, while the amount of dividend announced as being paid may not have been amended.

It's also worth mentioning that any stocks you already have within your portfolio may be suffering from falling prices, too. If you bought them at reasonable prices originally and your dividend yields are still strong, you may want to consider hanging onto them

and riding out the market until it shows signs of recovery.

Know When It's Time to Sell

The objective of putting together a stock portfolio to earn income from dividends is to adopt a long-term "buy and hold" strategy. However, this doesn't always mean you need to hold stocks forever. There are times when selling good stocks makes sense. There are also times when it's wise to sell off any under-performing stocks.

While a falling market might represent some opportunities to buy great stocks at reduced prices, it can also be an indication to sell under-performing stocks within your portfolio. When a particular stock really isn't worth holding onto any longer, you need to know when to cut your losses and sell.

Remember, there should be absolutely no emotion in investing. This is about making an informed decision to benefit your portfolio and your overall dividend income.

Always monitor the performance of the stocks within your portfolio. Never be afraid to sell if a stock no longer offers you the performance you expect.

Should You Use Dollar Cost Averaging?

Dollar cost averaging is a particular investment strategy used by many professional investors. Unfortunately, it's not always the right strategy for dividend-yield investing.

Dollar cost averaging is all about investing the same amount of money regularly over a period of time into growing your portfolio. For example, say you commit to investing $100 per month every month for 12 months. When prices are low, you are able to buy more stocks with that same amount of money. However, when prices go up you end up buying fewer stocks with the same money.

For example, let's say you buy 100 shares of ABC stock for $60, another 100 shares at

$65 and another 100 shares at $70. Your average cost for those shares will be $65.

For those people with only small amounts of money to invest, this can be an excellent way to gradually build up a portfolio over time. It allows you to work on setting up a regular savings plan and then put that money to good use over time as you can afford it. If you're buying a range of well-considered stocks throughout this time, you should find that you end up with a well-rounded, diversified portfolio of income-producing stocks.

Unfortunately, dollar cost averaging is all about buying exactly the same stocks every month, regardless of market conditions or prices.

For those with larger amounts to invest, dollar cost averaging over a period of time could potentially limit your investment. This is because only a small amount of money is being invested on a regular basis.

Statistics show that investors able to invest $1,200 up front are more likely to end up with a better rate of return overall in the following 12 month period as compared to those investors who choose to invest $100 per month over the same 12 month period.

Here's the formula:

Average Price Per Share = total cost of buying shares divided by number of shares

The whole point of doing this is to attempt to reduce the total average cost per share within your portfolio, which is intended to give you a lower total cost for those stocks you bought over that 12 month period. This lower total cost is intended to help limit your risk during market downturns.

It can also be helpful if you're trying to work out where to set your stop-loss order. If you know in this instance your average share price is $65, you might want to set your stop-loss order to 20% below this amount, which is $52. If your stock prices fall to this

amount, it may be time to consider selling out and cutting your losses.

Always Use Stop Loss Orders

Within your brokerage account you should have access to placing stop-loss orders. No matter how safe or risk-free you think a particular stock might be, there will always be circumstances that can cause you to lose money.

Setting stop-loss orders are vital to any successful investing strategy. They allow you to:

* Protect against further losses

* Help to lock in gains

A stop-loss order is an automatic order that is triggered whenever a stock reaches a pre-determined price that you can set. For example, you might buy stocks that cost you $30 per share. After a week, the price may have gone up to $40 per share. You're able to set a stop-loss order for $35, so if the stock's price falls below this price they'll

automatically be sold and you still keep your profit of $5 per share.

This is ideal for a short-term investor or an active trader, but it's not always the right approach for a long term investor. As your goal is to maintain a strong portfolio of stocks, you may want to set your stop-loss order to 20% or even 25% below the target price.

The reason for this is that the daily price fluctuations within the stock market shouldn't be your primary focus. It's only when really major pricing movements threaten your stock holdings that you should consider liquidating any long-term stocks you hold in your portfolio.

Types of Stop-Loss Orders

There are two primary types of stop-loss orders to remember: Market Orders and Limit Orders.

Limit Order

A Limit Order is when you set your sale price for your stocks to sell at a specific amount. For example, you may have purchased your stocks at $30 per share, but you could set your Limit Order to exactly $45 per share. It may take a while for the market to reach this limit, but when it does your order will go in. Unfortunately, there is a risk that Limit Orders may not be filled. This is especially true if the market is moving particularly quickly and the price shoots right past it on its way down.

Market Order

A Market Order is a little different in that your stocks will automatically be put on the market once the stocks reach the predetermined price you entered. So, if you've set your stop-loss Market Order to $45 and the market is still moving, you may not get exactly $45. Instead, you might get

$44.90 or a price that is relatively close to where you set your stop-loss order.

Within your brokerage account you should notice the option to select the type of stop-loss order you want to place. You should stick to Market Orders when possible.

You also should remember that your stop-loss limits can be amended and updated at any time as well. This is excellent if your original stop-loss order was set at $45 but the market is still climbing at the stock price is now at $55 per share. You can reset your stop-loss order for $50 and know that you've protected your gains as the prices continue to rise.

Growing Your Stock Portfolio

The whole objective of this book is to show you how to create an income from dividends. However, in order to build your portfolio to a large enough size to produce a healthy income, you first need to grow it.

There are several ways to increase the size of your stock portfolio. You can:

* Invest more of your own money

* Wait for the stock prices to rise

* Re-invest your dividends

If you're serious about generating a realistic dividend income, you may want to work on all three of these options. Let's look at them all in some more detail.

Invest More of Your Own Money

If you're already on a tight budget and really don't have a large amount of money to invest, you can start out with a very small amount and still build up a strong portfolio easily. We mentioned this in a previous chapter, but it does bear repeating.

It's completely up to you how you manage your household budget, but if your goal is to earn money from dividends it's probably a wise idea to think about finding ways to cut your current expenses a little. When you

can put aside enough money to buy more stocks, go ahead and place your trade order.

As mentioned previously, even $100 is enough to buy you 4 stocks at $25 per share. Of course, if you have more to invest then you'll find it a little easier to get started with larger amounts.

You also have the option of using a brokerage that allows you to invest as little as $25 per week to get started with your investing. This lets you put aside money on a regular basis that is then invested into growing your portfolio on a regular basis. Along with other portfolio-growth options, this has the potential to seriously grow your investment value to many times more than you paid for it over time.

Wait for Prices to Rise

This strategy is not always a good way to build any portfolio as stock prices can – and

do – fall. Besides, putting all your hopes on the prospect of capital gains on stocks you've bought is a bit like gambling.

However, it's always a good idea to keep an eye on your overall portfolio value and individual stock prices.

Re-Invest Your Dividends

During the growth phase of building your stock portfolio, it's important to search for corporations that will allow you to re-invest your dividends. You want your dividends paid to you in the form of additional stocks added to your portfolio.

This approach means you will not be earning any cash payments from the dividends you earn at first. Instead, those dividend earnings will be buying you more stocks to add to your existing portfolio.

What's more, you're not paying any commissions or brokerage fees to have those additional stocks added to your holdings. This represents a saving to you, as

buying those same stocks with your own money would have cost you those fees and charges.

As long as you're in the growth phase of your investing plan, always work on re-investing your dividends and receiving your payments in the form of more stock. As your stock holdings grow, the amount you earn from dividends will also grow. You may also find that the overall value of your stock portfolio increases as a result.

The longer you hold stocks within your portfolio, the more your returns are able to compound.

Imagine starting your portfolio owning only 20 shares of a strong, well-performing stock. After 10 years, your number of shares in that company could have grown to 2,200 shares – and that's without adding any of your own extra money. That's just the power of re-investing the dividends you earn and allowing the returns to compound.

When you add in the power of compounding growth, you suddenly have a strong portfolio that is increasing in value. At the same time, the number of stocks you own is increasing on its own, which further increases your dividend income. It's at this point you can choose to continue re-investing your dividends or switch it over to cash dividends and use it as your own income.

Leveraging for Growth

Once you have built up your stock portfolio a little, some brokerages will allow you to borrow money against your share ownership. This type of lending is called margin lending, and it's designed to let you borrow a certain percentage of the value of the stocks you own in order to buy even more stocks.

The idea of leveraging your existing portfolio isn't a new idea. However, it is one that should be used with caution. Borrowing money for the purpose of investing in the

stock market can be fraught with danger. This is especially true if you leverage too highly or if you're not careful about how much you're borrowing.

Essentially, by borrowing some funds against the value of your existing shares, you have the opportunity to purchase even more.

The key to succeeding with this principle is to work out the calculations for how much your interest repayments will cost you on your margin loan and then work out how much extra you'll earn in dividend payments as a result.

For example: let's assume you have a portfolio with a value of $10,000. You may decide to borrow at a 40% loan to value ratio. This gives you an additional $4,000 to invest into the market.

Assuming you buy stocks that return 8% dividend yield, this gives you $320 per year in additional dividend income from just those new stocks you purchased. Of course,

you also still have your initial $10,000 portfolio earning dividends as well. This is a total of $14,000 earning dividend income. Let's assume your total portfolio is returning 6% on average. This means you're earning around $840 a year in dividend income.

As your portfolio value grows, you have the ability to borrow even more money against it. This helps you boost your overall value, but it also raises how much you earn in dividends. As a result, if you stick to the dividend re-investment plan, you end up with far more stocks in your portfolio overall. And so it compounds again.

Unfortunately, margin loans are often charged at higher interest rates than home mortgages or personal loans. This is where it's important to work out exactly how much you'll repay on your margin loan. It's also vitally important to ensure you never borrow so much that your earnings don't quite cover the amount you need to repay.

Ideally, if you do borrow a small amount to increase your stock holdings, you should work out a way to repay your balance easily. This could mean using your own income to repay this amount, which also means keeping the balance within easily affordable levels. It could also mean strategically choosing one of your stocks to revert to cash dividends in order to use that cash to make repayments in advance as you receive it.

A Word of Warning about Margin Loans

Margin loans can seem like an easy way to increase your portfolio value and boost your dividend earnings at the same time. However, it's really important that you never leverage your borrowings too high.

The vast majority of brokerages will limit the amount you can borrow against your stock values to between 60% and 80%. This might be very tempting, but you'll be much safer to limit your borrowings to between

40% and 50% of the total value of your portfolio.

The reason for this is because stock prices do fluctuate. The market does rise and fall. If the market was to fall far enough that your stock values end up lower than your margin loan amount, you will officially go into "margin call".

A margin call is when your brokerage demands that you immediately reduce your outstanding loan amount down to an acceptable loan to value ratio. If you don't have the available cash to do this, your stocks will automatically be sold down in an effort to reduce your margin loan balance.

As margin calls most often happen during market downturns, this means the value of the stocks you're selling is also at a low point. You're getting less money for your stocks, the proceeds of which will then go to repaying your margin loan down to acceptable levels.

THE DIVIDEND MILLIONAIRE

This situation can be more easily avoided by being very cautious about the amount borrowed. Always take the time to work through calculations as thoroughly as you can before attempting this strategy.

Going From Portfolio Growth to Dividend Income

During the growth phase of your portfolio, you really need to focus hard on dividend re-investment, plus adding additional funds from your own income whenever you can afford to do so. This will keep your level of stock holdings rising, which should result in an increased portfolio value.

However, the whole object of doing this is to create an income from the dividends you earn. This is where you need to have grown your portfolio to such a level that the income earned is substantial enough to supplement your income, or even replace it.

Just as you nominated to re-invest your dividends initially to grow your portfolio value, you can also nominate to return to

cash dividend payments when it suits you. From this point, you're able to use that cash income how you choose.

Always check with your accountant how this might affect your taxable income overall. In fact, it's very wise to check with your accountant whether you need to declare your re-invested dividends as income as well.

Conclusion

Never believe that you don't have enough money to begin investing. The whole key to successful investing is starting with whatever you have. Once you've begun, work out a way to regularly add even small amounts to your existing portfolio. This might mean investing as little as $25 a week just to get you into a positive investing schedule. It might also mean re-arranging your budget and your income to work out a way to afford to put aside more money.

Regardless of your options, the sooner you get started the sooner you'll be able to begin compounding your initial efforts to start building up your stock portfolio. As your dividend earnings are re-invested back into adding more stocks to your portfolio, your overall value increases. At the same time, the amount of dividends you earn will also increase.

As long as you stick to a simple strategy, you should see very positive results. The longer you hold to your strategy and monitor your portfolio, the better your overall dividend income will be.

What's more, you're not just earning a good income from your dividends. You're also working on a solid wealth creation strategy, as your overall portfolio still has its own value. While you might think a few extra thousand dollars a year in dividend growth sounds like fun, owning a stock portfolio worth tens of thousands, or even hundreds of thousands of dollars can certainly put you

closer to your goal of becoming a dividend millionaire.

Spend some time researching good quality, solid stocks that return good dividend yields. Then work on a way to get started sooner rather than later.

Have You Read?

Economic Crisis: Surviving Global Currency Collapse - Safeguard Your Financial Future with Silver and Gold.

Clearly, investing in silver and gold will help protect your assets in the event of a currency collapse. While many people claim this can't happen, there are just as many signs pointing to it as a serious possibility. If global currency collapse does occur, you will need to have some form of wealth protection in place that not only ensures you are protecting the value of your assets but can also be converted into everyday

items you will need. That's why it's best to have something of value to trade and nothing is more valuable than investment gold and silver bullions – The Real Money.

This book and others are available in print at most online retailers.

Your capital is at risk when you invest in stocks - you can lose some or all of your money, so never risk more than you can afford to lose. Always seek professional advice if you are unsure about the suitability of any investment. Past performance is not a reliable indicator of future results.

Printed in Great Britain
by Amazon